IMAGES
of England

SALE AND SALE MOOR

IMAGES
of England

SALE AND SALE MOOR

Jan Shearsmith, Karen Cliff
Vicki Masterson, Pat Southern

TEMPUS

John Brogden was born in the Furness district of Lancashire and married in 1822, settling in the Manchester area with his family. He was the founder of John Brogden & Sons, a railway construction company, and was the contractor for the Manchester to Altrincham section of the Manchester South Junction and Altrincham Railway. John was a prominent Wesleyan in the Sale area and in 1854 purchased the 'Bridge chapel' from the Congregationalists for the sum of £400, which he then presented to the Wesleyans so that they could alleviate the problem of overcrowding they had at their Broad Lane chapel.

Frontispiece: James Joule was born in Salford but lived in Wardle Road, Sale, during the latter part of his life. He won many awards for his pioneering work in the field of thermodynamics including the Copley medal (1870), the Blue Ribbon of Engineering Science (1852) and the Royal Society Blue Medal (1880). He is most famous for his work involving the mechanical equivalent of heat and the figure 772.55 appears on his memorial in Brooklands c emetery.

First published 2002

Tempus Publishing Limited
The Mill, Brimscombe Port,
Stroud, Gloucestershire, GL5 2QG

British Library Cataloguing in Publication Data.
A catalogue record for this book is available from the British Library.

ISBN 0 7524 2485 8

Typesetting and origination by Tempus Publishing Limited
Printed in Great Britain by Midway Colour Print, Wiltshire

Contents

School Road in 1913.

Bibliography

Bennett, G.H. *Twenty Five Years of Urban Growth in Sale*, (unpublished typescript).
Borough of Sale, *Charter Celebration September 21 1935*,1935.
Burke, Wilfred *Reminiscences of Sale* (unpublished manuscript), 1944.
Hainsworth, Vivian *Looking Back at Sale*, 1983.
Newhill, John *The Story of Sale from 1806 to 1876: a house detective book*, 2000.
Sale, Cheshire in 1841: its people in their lives, 1994.
Swain, Norman *A History of Sale: from earliest times to the present day*, 1987.
Wesley Chapel Sale, Official Handbook.
Guardian Yearbook, miscellaneous dates.
Slater's Directory, miscellaneous dates.
Trafford MBC, Local History Pack on Sale, Altrincham, Hale and Bowdon miscellaneous dates.
Guardian Trafford Local Studies, Ephemera and pamphlet collection.

Introduction and Acknowledgements

This book is not intended to be a comprehensive or definitive history of Sale and Sale Moor, but it is designed to provide glimpses of the past using the photographs from the collection at Trafford Local Studies Centre. The assemblage in this book is one means of promoting the local studies library service, with the open invitation to visit the Local Studies Centre if more information is required. There is an extensive collection of maps and plans, books, pamphlets and around 20,000 photographs in stock at the Local Studies Centre, covering the whole Borough of Trafford; and about one quarter of this material concerns the Sale area. In some cases the photographs in this book have already been published in other books on Sale, but the authors make no apology for using them again, since there have been relatively few books on the history of Sale, most are out of print, and there is sometimes no other alternative photograph in the library stock. For those photographs which are published here for the first time, every care had been taken to trace copyright owners for those which have been donated to the library. Since photography is a relatively young art, being a phenomenon of the 1840s onwards, the emphasis in this book is on the nineteenth century and later.

Anyone who studies the history of Sale needs to use the late Norman Swain's *A History of Sale*, which is now sadly out of print, as is Vivien Hainsworth's *Looking Back at Sale*. The authors are grateful to these fellow authors for their pioneering work, and to several people for their ready co-operation in granting the right to use their photographs, or ideas from their published works. These include: Mr Colin Sykes, Mr John Newhill, David and Gill Fitzpatrick, Mr Doug Rendell and Dr Mike Nevell. They are not responsible for any errors in this book; these remain the responsibility of the authors, who can be contacted at Trafford Local Studies Centre.

Pat Southern
Local Studies Librarian
Trafford Local Studies Centre
May 2002

Portrait of Dr Charles White, one of the principal landowners of Sale. His father Thomas bought Sale Priory, and Charles was born and grew up in Sale. He went on to become a distinguished surgeon. He was a fellow of the Royal Society, and a member of the Royal College of Surgeons.

One

Rural Sale

Driving through Sale today, nose-to-tail at a rush-hour maximum of five miles per hour, it is hard to visualize the once open aspect of the land and the small farms that made up the area before industrialization changed the face of the whole of the Manchester conurbation. Early maps show that until the second half of the nineteenth century the settlements of Sale and Ashton upon Mersey were little more than villages, surrounded by fields. Bounded on the north by the Mersey, Sale came to a ragged end at the flood plain of the river, a feature which largely determined the extent of settlement and the type of agriculture in the area.

The early history of Sale is not documented, and thus remains a matter for speculation and guesswork, based on comparison with other areas. The presence of the Roman road, which forms the boundary between Sale and Ashton on Mersey, attests to 400 years of Roman occupation, but nothing at all has come to light to suggest that Romano-British farms may have existed on or near the road. Nor are the Anglo-Saxons represented, except perhaps in the place name Sale, which is said to derive from an Anglo-Saxon word, *sealh*, which means willow. This is entirely possible, since the area is close to the river Mersey and may have supported willow trees along the banks. The Normans did not record Sale in the Domesday Book, but this does not mean that there was no settlement in the area. There could have been a few inhabitants who were included in the administration of one of the nearby manors.

Next to nothing is known of the medieval farms in Sale. The general pattern in much of medieval England was open field strip farming, usually with three unhedged or unfenced fields, two of which were cultivated in any one year, and the third lying fallow. The fallow and cultivated fields were rotated each year to give the soil time to regenerate its fertility. In the area around Sale, this generalized picture may have been slightly different, in that there was more pasture land suitable for cattle rearing and dairy farming. So the medieval inhabitants of Sale may have operated a system of mixed farming, growing crops in strip fields, but also pasturing cattle on the grass lands and reaping the hay crops to feed the animals through the winter. Each household cultivated several different strips, usually with a communal plough team of oxen. The strips were made up of soil heaped up in the centre, with a gully between each strip, which aided drainage. The term for this type of cultivation is ridge and furrow, which describes exactly what the fields looked like. Where evidence survives in the landscape, the fields look like pieces of corduroy, especially from the air. See Norman Swain, *A History of Sale: from earliest times to the present day*, for a photograph of ridge and furrow seen from the ground. As time went on during the medieval period, people would swap neighbouring strips in order to create larger blocks of cultivable land. This process may be visible on some of the older maps of Sale, where long narrow fields are shown, for instance on the 1806 enclosure map and the Tithe map of 1844.

Most medieval manors had access to common grazing lands where the peasants were entitled to pasture their animals, and some were surrounded by wastelands that were gradually converted to arable or pasture. As early as the thirteenth century, lords of the manors began to enclose some of this land, and acts were passed to ensure that the tenants still had access to sufficient pasture for their beasts. From the seventeenth century onwards, more and more land was enclosed, sometimes by private agreement, but more often by a private act passed through Parliament. A general enclosure act was passed in 1801 to facilitate the procedure, because the passage of private acts was beginning to clog the Parliamentary system, and also in that period it was vital to increase agricultural production because of the pressures of the Napoleonic Wars.

For the history of Sale, the 1801 act held great importance, since four years later in 1805, an act was passed to enclose lands in Sale Moor. From a historian's point of view the map that was drawn to illustrate the enclosures provides a very rare insight into the town's history. The map shows the size and shape of each field, and an accompanying survey reference book gives the names of the landowners and the occupiers of the farms, together with the names of the fields, much like the later Tithe map. In general terms, a glance at the 1806 map reveals two different field patterns; with the older long, narrow fields in the west, in Sale itself, and the newly enclosed areas in the east and the south east, where the fields are larger and more or less square, in Sale Moor. This is the usual pattern for late eighteenth and early nineteenth century enclosure.

The reduction of common lands meant that the poor who were accustomed to pasture their animals there were forced to find alternative work, and often had to become labourers for the larger landowners, or for various tradespeople. The early landowners were the Masseys, who owned half of the manor of Sale, and then from the eighteenth century the Leghs of High Legh, who inherited the Massey lands. The other half of the manor of Sale was owned by the Booths of Dunham Massey, who bought the land in the early seventeenth century. Their part of Sale was passed on to the Stamfords when the Booths died out. In his book *The Story of Sale from 1806 to 1876,* John Newhill was able to show that the noble landowning families, who owned much of Sale and Sale Moor in 1806, had declined in importance by the 1840s, and instead new landowning families emerged, such as that of Samuel Brooks. Between 1804 and 1844, property ownership of all categories increased, especially the smaller properties under 20 acres.

Up to the mid-nineteenth century the majority of people in Sale were farmers or market gardeners. The maps of Sale reveal that many farms were accompanied by glass houses, where nursery produce was grown. One of Sale's most famous crops was rhubarb, the closest rival for this produce being Timperley; many people remember 'Timperley early' rhubarb in the markets.

The farms gradually disappeared as the transport revolution changed the way in which people lived and worked. The arrival of the railway in the second half of the ninteenth century brought more and more people to the area, as new houses were erected on the old farm lands. Some of the farms were sold and their lands amalgamated with other farms, but eventually they too disappeared. Unfortunately for historians, the development of photography and photographic habit had not been fully established before the farms of Sale started to disappear. So unlike the Urmston and Flixton areas where the housing schemes came much later,s after the Manchester Ship Canal opened, there are few photographss of rural Sale and the farms that occupied the present built up areas. By the end of the nineteenth century, farming and market gardening had largely given way to suburbanization. Only about a dozen farms are listed in the directories from around 1900 to 1930, including Moor Nook Farm; Temple Farm; Ivy Farm on Dane Road; Heys Farm, Raglan Road; New Farm, Washway Road; Beech Farm, Baguley Road; Moss Farm, Moss Lane; Manor Farm at No. 112 Cross Street and Old Hall Farm, Old Hall Road. By 1939 only about five of these were remaining.

An undated map from the nineteenth century already shows the building on what was the wasteland in the centre of Sale. This map clearly shows that Sale was as yet comparatively untouched by industry or the suburban sprawl as it spread out from Manchester.

Sale was still a partly rural area as late as 1904. In the distance can be seen the police station, which still stands at the corner of Tatton Road and Tatton Place.

Ash Farm, Ashton Lane, 1939. It was demolished to make room for modern housing.

Fiddler's Farm, Firs Road, *c*. 1877.

Ashton Hall Farm, *c*. 1920.

Ashton Old Hall Farm, at the end of the nineteenth century.

New Farm, Washway Road, 1937. Mr John Arthur Garner is leading his horse called Prince with a loaded cart.

Moss Farm in 1963 just before the compulsory purchase order came into effect to demolish the property to make way for the Manor Road development.

The Garners of New Farm, at Smithfield Market, Manchester, where they went each week to sell their produce.

Cherry Lane, 1963, with Natt Hall Farm, the subject of a compulsory purchase order as plans to erect houses were formed.

Left: Close to the boundary with Northenden is Norris Road, originally known as Essex Road. This picture was taken in the early 1900s, and clearly shows the rural nature of Sale at the turn of the century. *Right:* Wellfield Nursery in Dumber Lane, Ashton on Mersey, where the Yarwood family ran their market garden business. Before moving to the nursery the Yarwoods can be found living at No. 58 Old Hall Road in the 1891 census returns.

Fir Bob Farm, on Firs Road, now Firsway. The farm was demolished when the housing estate was built.

Left: Wellfield Nursery in the early 1900s; John Yarwood can be seen in the background with his brother Samuel at work in one of the greenhouses. The Ordnance Survey map of the area shows it as fields until 1910. The 1901 census return shows the Yarwood family living there. *Right:* Another picture of John Yarwood, standing on the left. Before moving to Ashton on Mersey, the Yarwoods lived close to the Sale Green area. When the family first moved there they lived at No. 17 St Ann's Street in 1871 and 1881.

According to the notes included with this picture the young man guiding the plough is Harold Barrett and the horse is Dolly from Royle's Bakery.

Left: Sarah Yarwood with her daughter Ellen. Sarah was married to William, a blacksmith, and the family can be found in the 1861 census living at Hart Lane. This is now Northenden Road, close to the boundary with Northenden. *Right:* Sarah Yarwood during the 1940s.

The rear view of Wellfield Nurseries showing the extensive green houses.

Since flowers require pollination by insects, the Yarwoods kept bees at the nursery. This photograph shows John Yarwood inspecting their extensive collection of hives. The varied construction of the hives shows that no material was regarded as unsuitable.

Sale Green in 1895, looking down Broad Road, with the smithy on the left and various horse-drawn vehicles in the distance

A later view of Sale Green and the smithy, around 1900, with a horse-drawn bus in the distance on Old Hall Road.

John Yarwood, seated on the right, was the owner of the Broad Road smithy.

There were many family-run nurseries in the area, Henry Brownhill being another such family concern.

Shoeing a horse at the smithy on Broad Road.

Potato warehouse situated in Chapel Lane, as used by Cowan's when this photograph was taken. Tradition has it that this was the site of the old Pinfold which John Newhill mentions in his book *Sale, Cheshire, in 1841*.

Sale Old Hall, which stood on the south side of Rifle Road, photographed here during the First World War. There is potential for confusion in the halls of Sale, since the Old Hall and the New Hall have both been rebuilt at least once. The Old Hall was rebuilt in the 1840s, but there has been a property situated on this site since the 1600s. The Massey family owned it, but their line came to an end and the Old Hall eventually came into the possession of Mary Worthington. Norman Swain says in his *History of Sale* that 'The Hall was over two centuries old at the time and its condition may have been such, that Mrs Worthington had no other option than to demolish and rebuild'. The 1840s house shown here served as a convalescent home for casualties from the First World War, and was then demolished in the 1920s.

Sale Old Hall has had many inhabitants, apart from the Massey family and Mrs Mary Worthington. In 1888 it was the home of Sir William Bailey, a prominent Manchester businessman during the late 1800s.

Left: A later addition to the Old Hall was the Dovecote, which still stands. It is not known precisely when it was built; Swain suggests 1895, since the building is not marked on the first edition Ordnance Survey map of 1874, and first appears of the map of 1897. This picture was taken in the 1960s. *Right:* The Dovecote. This particular picture was taken in 1972 during the construction of the M60 motorway.

Sale New Hall on Fairy Lane was built, according to the date stone above the door, in 1688 for William Massey. The building was used for several purposes; it was at one time a farm, and at another it was divided into cottages. Sale New Hall was demolished in 1953. According to reports by the Senior Sanitary Inspector and the Medical Officer of Health it was unfit for human habitation.

Two

Transport

In Sale, transport history is exciting, because there are so many 'firsts' – the early Roman road, the first canal in England, one of the first steam railways, and the first electric passenger railway service which all pass through Sale.

For many centuries the horse was the main means of transport, for traction for vehicles or for riding, so the distance that anyone could travel in one day was extremely limited by modern standards. Even when other forms of transport were in operation, such as canal boats and railways, the horse was still necessary to transport people and goods from the wharves and railways stations until motorized transport ousted the horse from its prime position in society.

The canals were hailed as a revolutionary concept, enabling heavy goods to be transported relatively quickly and with little horsepower. One horse could pull a laden barge with ease, and when the first industrialists realized that raw materials could be brought in, and finished goods could be distributed by the canal system, various factories and businesses were established by the canals or within easy reach of them. The first sections of the Bridgewater canal were opened in 1759, providing the basis for development all along the route, which eventually ran from Worsley to Runcorn. The Sale sections of the canal were constructed after the Act of Parliament was passed in 1762, authorizing the Duke of Bridgewater to 'make, complete and maintain a navigable Cut or Canal, passable for boats, barges, and other vessels, at all times and seasons, from or near Longford Bridge... over the river Mersey and through the several townships of Altringham, Dunham... Lym and Thelwell, in the county of Chester, and to or near a certain place called the Hemp Stones, in or near the township of Halton'. The Act also specified that the Duke was authorized to cut trenches, remove earth and rubble, and to 'construct, erect and keep in repair any piers, arches and other works, in, upon, and across the river Mersey, between the said Longford Bridge and Altringham'. The Act stipulated that no corn mills were to be erected on the canal banks or the towing paths. Tolls were established for the goods carried on the barges, 'not exceeding the sum of two shillings and sixpence for every ton of coal, stone, timber and other goods, wares, merchandizes and commodities'. Coal was one of the most important commodities handled on the Bridgewater at Sale.

The photographs in this chapter show all kinds of horse-drawn vehicles, two wheeled, four wheeled, drawn by single horses or by teams, privately owned vehicles, hired vehicles and public passenger services. The larger vehicles such as horse buses and horse trams had a relatively short life before being overtaken by electric-powered trams and motor buses. Horse-drawn buses operated from around 1830 until the 1870s, with the limitations that any horse transport put on them, namely the small number of passengers that could be carried in any one vehicle, and the fact that long journeys required frequent stops and changes of horses. From the end of the 1870s powered trams began to take over the horse tram lines, though in Stretford the horses were still used as late as 1903. This was pending the establishment of powered trams, which had already been agreed on between Manchester and Stretford Urban District in 1900. There was a long delay before the electric cars were up and running into Stretford, and it was not until 1906 that the first trams ran into Sale. Six years later the first trams began to operate in Sale Moor, as far as the Legh Arms.

The main changes in Sale were brought about not by the arrival of the canal, nor the advent of horse-drawn buses, but by the railway. In 1830 the line from Liverpool to Manchester opened, and a decade later there were several other lines running into and out of Manchester, but none of the termini were linked up. The Manchester and South Junction line was originally built to link up two of the individual terminus stations so that passengers could travel on to Liverpool. Then it was decided to build a branch line, extending the Manchester and South Junction to Altrincham. In July 1845 the plan was approved, receiving royal assent, and work started in October 1845. The contract to build the Altrincham line with its bridges and stations was given to John Brogden of Sale, who only a short time before had objected to the coming of the railway because it was thought that the new transport system would be detrimental to Sale. Depending on one's point of view, perhaps it was, since it brought the rapid development of housing, and the obliteration of the farms in the area as more and more land was taken up for building. Commuting was born, and the Manchester factory owners and their workers could now live some short distance away from the city, and live in a pleasant suburb. The housing that we see today in Sale owes its origins to the invention of relatively cheap and fast transport, and the foresight of the planners, builders and engineers who made the railway possible. The original station building at Sale was only very small, and it was not until 1874 that the present brick edifice was founded. Schemes for the electrification of railway lines began in the 1920s, because by then the electric-powered trams had begun to compete with the trains, especially since the trams delivered people to the town centres, while the railways could only drop their passengers off at the designated stations. In 1928 the movement towards national electric railways was finalized when the Ministry of Transport recommended the use of overhead cables using a 1,500 volt DC system. The committee of the Manchester South Junction and Altrincham Railway had also been investigating electrification, and decided upon this system. Construction began in 1929, and the first electric train passed through Sale on the journey from Manchester to Altrincham on 14 April 1931. Journey times were cut, and more trains were put on during the day, thus increasing the attractions of living in Sale, only 15 to 20 minutes away from the centre of Manchester.

The motorized transport revolution is a comparatively recent development, but its growth has been very rapid. For special excursions the early tour operators used their charabancs, looking a little like stretch limos today, but with more doors. These vehicles could carry several people, but not as many as the public service motor buses, which found their niche in the 1920s and 1930s. A bus service between Altrincham and Manchester and running through Sale was operated by Manchester Corporation during the 1930s, and eventually the North Western Road Car Company Ltd absorbed many of the smaller firms from its establishment in 1923, at King Edward Street, Macclesfield. Two coach companies were based in Sale, Sykes Motor Tours Ltd at No. 180 Washway Road, and from 1972 Godfrey Abbott set up their office on Cross Street. In 1937, Sykes Tours advertised a return trip to Blackpool, setting off at 8.54 a.m., for the sum of six shillings and threepence. The journey to Rhyl took longer and cost more – ten shillings for the return trip, about fifty pence in modern currency. Although that seems ridiculously cheap, it would take quite a long time at work to earn ten shillings in 1937.

The river Mersey forms a natural obstacle to traffic going in a northerly or southerly direction between Stretford and Sale. There was probably a ferry at or near the point where Crossford Bridge now traverses the Mersey, and according to Swain's *History of Sale*, a bridge had been built by 1538. It was repaired or rebuilt in 1577, and it may have been destroyed in 1745, to stop the progress of the Scots as Bonnie Prince Charlie swept into England in an attempt to usurp the throne. In order to provide an income for the upkeep of the road surfaces and bridges, tolls were levied on major roads in the eighteenth and nineteenth centuries. This photograph shows Crossford Bridge toll house and gate, at an unknown date, but it must have been prior to 31 October 1885, because the toll bar was officially closed on that date.

Another view of Crossford Bridge toll gate from the opposite direction, as the hay cart (seen above) passes through. The road surface is fairly muddy, but in good condition, and there are raised pavements on either side of the route.

A postcard, dated 1927, shows a tram on Crossford Bridge.

Another crossing point on the river Mersey was at Jackson's Bridge, at the eastern end of Rifle Road. It is an inextricable part of Sale's history, though administratively it lies within the city of Manchester. This photograph, taken in the 1880s, shows the Bridge Inn, better known as Jackson's Boat, or Jackson's Ferry Boat, which gives a clue as to how the Mersey used to be crossed before the bridge was built. The ferry was made redundant when a wooden bridge was built in 1816. After a severe storm which swept the first bridge away, an iron bridge replaced the wooden one in 1881. Jackson's Ferry Boat Inn is said to have been a regular meeting place in the eighteenth century for Jacobites who supported the claims of Bonny Prince Charlie to the throne. The members of the Jacobite club used to salute the King, but raised their glasses over a bowl of water in the middle of the table – the secret sign that they were really saluting 'the King over the water', in exile in France. The building shown here is not the original inn, though parts of the early building may have been incorporated into the new one.

Horse-drawn vehicles near the fountain, Ashton upon Mersey. Drinking water for the horses along the routes would be very important, almost the equivalent of modern petrol stations.

Before the introduction of the railways and motorized transport, horse-drawn vehicles of many different types provided the only rapid transport, for both private and public use. Here can be seen a horse and two-wheeled covered trap, with a group of onlookers, on Ashton Lane around the turn of the nineteenth and twentieth centuries.

A well-groomed pony pulling a trap on Carrington Lane in the 1920s. The name J.H. Hayman is painted on the side of the trap. Street directories of the period list J.H. Hayman, coal merchant, White Gate Farm, Carrington Lane, Ashton on Mersey.

A single-decker horse bus with space for luggage on top, in Sale Moor village, between 1900 and 1910. Horse-drawn buses operated in most areas of Trafford in the nineteenth century before the introduction of powered vehicles. The ride would be somewhat uncomfortable as the horse buses were noted for jolting on the rough road surfaces. When trams were introduced, running on smooth level tracks, the passengers had a much more comfortable journey.

A two-decker horse bus in Sale, *c.* 1900. The design derives from the old stagecoaches, with an additional deck built on top.

Horse-drawn hearse in Sale in the early 1900s.

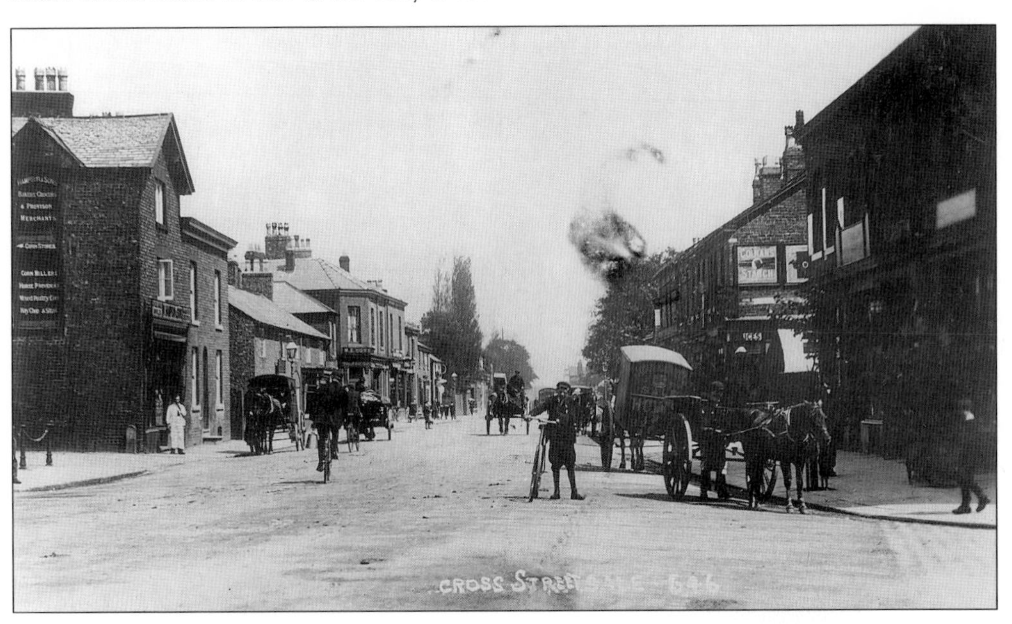

Several varieties of horse-drawn transport on Cross Street, around 1900-1910.

A splendid coach and horses passing the Waggon and Horses Hotel.

The Bridgewater Canal at Sale, with Chapel Road running alongside it, around 1875-1880. The Bridgewater Canal was opened in 1759 and provided the basis for industrial development all along the route from Worsley to Runcorn. There were wharves all along the eastern side of the canal, some of them connecting with goods yards and depots of the Manchester South Junction and Altrincham Railway. One of the main commodities carried on the canal was coal. The name Bridgewater Colliery is painted on the wheeled cart in this photograph, and a street directory of 1899 lists the Wigan Coal and Iron Company Ltd, coal owners (William Hamnett, agent), on Chapel Street.

Sale station photographed in 1880 or a little earlier, showing cobbled street and forecourt. The station master from 1898 until around 1904 was Richard Wardleworth; from 1905-1909 Samuel Lambert took over, and from 1910 until 1916 and later, it was the turn of Thomas Warburton.

Another view of Sale station in the 1890s. The horse and two-wheeled cart, and the horse and cab waiting by the lamp post, extreme left, indicates that there was still a demand for horse transport when the railway was established, to deliver goods brought by rail and to take people to their homes, just as motorized taxis queue up outside stations today.

Sale Bridge after widening, *c.* 1913. Note the telegraph poles bristling with terminals for the wires. The building just glimpsed over the centre of the bridge is the Bridgewater coal office.

The lines at Sale station, looking towards Manchester, *c.* 1870. The project for the Manchester South Junction and Altrincham Railway was begun in the 1840s. The line was surveyed in 1844 and was approved by the Crown in July 1845. The contract to build the Altrincham section of the line was granted to John Brogden of Sale. Only a few months before he won the contract, John Brogden had added his name to the list of signatures objecting to the railway! At the Sale Township Meeting held on 2 January 1845, it was resolved that the proposed railway would be 'very prejudicial and injurious to Property, Roads, and Public Highways within this township'. The railway opened for passengers on Friday, 20 July 1849, only nineteen years after the Liverpool and Manchester Railway was established, changing the face of transport forever.

Waiting for a train on Sale station, *c.* 1900. A steam engine can be glimpsed in the distance.

Alighting from a train at Brooklands in 1981. In stark contrast to the days of the steam trains the electric wiring can be seen overhead. The line was first electrified in 1931, and this photograph was taken to mark the fiftieth anniversary of the event.

Sale Bridge just before the road was widened, 1912. The bridges over the railway were all designed by John Brogden.

Open-topped tram passing the Volunteer Hotel on Cross Street, probably around 1908, though the photograph was undated. The tram service to Sale was established in 1906, as an extension of the Manchester to Stretford line.

After the success of the 1906 tramline to Sale, a tram route was extended into Sale Moor. Seen here are the cutting of the lines in Sale Moor village, in March 1912.

On 4 July 1912, the first passenger vehicles began to operate. Seen here is the first car, traveling along Northenden Road and entering Sale Moor Village, very early in the morning. This may explain why there were only a few onlookers, and perhaps only two dedicated photographers, the one shown in the right foreground, and the unseen one who took this picture.

Tram on route No. 49, in floods on Cross Street. The route was taken over by motor buses and renumbered 117. The photograph was taken from negatives lent by Mrs D. Vickers.

By the summer of 1912 the first tramcars were running and seen here is an open-topped special car on the first official run into Sale Moor village in June 1912.

Several forms of transport are seen here – horse and cart, tram and motorized coal lorry on Cross Street in floods. The exact date is uncertain, but the tram in the distance has a closed top, which was not introduced until 1904, the lines were not laid into Sale until 1906, and experts date the lorry to post 1908.

Motorized transport began to make an impression in the early twentieth century, though not on the scale that we see in Sale today. This photograph from around 1908 shows the passengers lined up, ready for a 'gentleman's outing' by charabanc, departing from the Volunteer Hotel on Cross Street.

Sale Bridge with a horse-drawn cart, a closed-top tram coming from the town hall and a bicycle rider.

A charabanc about to set off on the Chapel Road tenants' outing to Blackpool or Morecambe, c. 1922.

A solitary motor car on Buck Lane in the 1930s.

The advent of motorized transport demanded smoother road surfaces and constant repairs. Road menders are shown here at the cab stand on Northenden Road in the 1900s. The area was colloquially known as Cat's Park.

This splendid vehicle is driven by James Whittaker, chauffeur to Fred Hardy of Tyntesfield.

Underneath the tarmac on many roads in Sale there are square stone sets, which made for a durable surface but an uncomfortable ride. Tar spraying can be seen here outside the Waggon and Horses in 1905.

One of the original Sykes coaches, probably in the late 1920s; note the curtains at the windows. Sykes Tours operated from Washway Road, opposite the Vine Inn.

Old and new style coaches at Sykes Tours, in the early 1930s.

Number 47 bus going to Sale, in the mid-1930s. This type of bus was used for nearly twenty years, first appearing in around 1934 and finally being scrapped in the 1950s.

Double-decker bus on Glebelands Road. Motor buses were more flexible than trams, not needing tram lines to run on, and so cornered the transport market.

Postcard view of Washway Road showing open-topped and closed-topped trams at the junction with Ashton Lane. Horses were still supreme on the roads at this time, motor cars were rare, and bicycles ran the risk of getting their tyres stuck in the tram lines.

Washway Road in 1950 with a few more motor cars and lorries, but still a far cry from modern usage.

Three

The Suburban Explosion

One of the most telling methods of documenting the growth of Sale is a study of the available maps of the nineteenth and early twentieth centuries. The Tithe map shows a rural area dotted with farms set in fields, with very few houses. The earliest large-scale Ordnance Survey map shows a cluster of buildings on either side of the railway station, on the south side of School Road and Northenden Road, where the nucleus of Sale can be discerned. However, towards the east, there were large fields with small groups of houses, mostly detached or semi-detached, along Northenden Road and the roads leading off it. By 1898, the pattern of housing had expanded. Encroachments had begun on the once open land between Broad Road and Northenden Road. A row of large houses had been built on the east side of Wardle Road, on land which had previously been largely empty of houses, and on the east side of the Bridgewater canal, many new semi-detached and terraced houses had been built. On the opposite side of the canal groups of terraced houses had sprung up in the years between 1874 and 1898, around Roebuck Lane and Albion Street. At the eastern end of Northenden Road near the Legh Arms, new streets such as Hampson Street, Alice Street and James Street had been laid out, and several new houses had been built. Leading off Marsland Road, Victoria Road and Victoria Drive had been established, lined with small groups of terraced housing.

The appearance of these new houses highlights the rapid growth of the population of Sale, and the clustering of the dwellings around or within easy reach of the railway station demonstrates the importance of the new form of transport in attracting new inhabitants to the area in the second half of the nineteenth century. In 1855, Sale was a township in the parish of Ashton upon Mersey, with only 1,720 inhabitants. The new railway station erected only a few years previously was called Sale Moor station, indicating that the territory beyond it still qualified in terminology if not in reality as open land. There was one church, St Anne's, built in 1854, and four chapels – one Independent chapel, the Primitive Methodist and the Wesleyan Methodist chapels, and one Presbyterian chapel. There were less than fifty names worthy of inclusion in the 'Gentry and Clergy' section of the directories, but despite the lack of population, education was well catered for, with three boarding schools, and also two schoolmasters whose premises are not listed. There were few businesses; apart from three coal companies with offices on or near the Bridgewater canal, there were only about seven grocery and general stores, two butchers, one draper and one milliner, and one blacksmith.

Though the population of Sale was still relatively small, it was recognized that there was a need to form a new parish for the inhabitants out of the parish of Ashton on Mersey, which was accomplished in 1856. By the 1890s the population had risen to 9,644, and with the rise in the numbers of inhabitants, the concomitant service industries and commercial premises had also increased. No post office is mentioned in 1855, but by 1864 there was a post and money order office on Cross Street and another post office at Sale Green. At the end of the nineteenth century there were three post offices, one on Washway Road, and two on Northenden Road. A police station had been established on Tatton Road, with one sergeant, Henry Beardsworth, in charge in the 1860s.

The Court of Petty Sessions was held in the police station every alternate Monday. In the 1890s the police establishment had expanded: there was one Inspector, George Ennion, assisted by three sergeants and fourteen constables. Another necessary service was the fire brigade, which was established in 1872. The fire engine house was at No. 4 School Road, with Walter Holmes as the superintendent in 1903; by 1915 Joseph Royle had taken over.

The town was growing in size and importance and required more complex organization and amenities. After the Local Government Act was passed in 1894, Sale Urban District Council was created, with fifteen members who governed the town meeting in the Council Room on School Road. By the beginning of the twentieth century the streets were lit by gas supplied by a company based in Stretford, and then by electric lighting from Trafford Power and Light Supply Ltd. Water and sewage works had been installed, operated by the North Cheshire Waterworks Company. The sewage works processed up to750,000 gallons per day in 1915, purified by chemical treatment and discharged direct into the river Mersey.

Education had always been a strong feature in Sale, beginning in the seventeenth century with a school built on common or waste land, but the site is not known; as Norman Swain points out, it could have been anywhere south of Broad Road. In the eighteenth century another school was established on Springfield Road, by converting two cottages for use as educational premises. Its successor was a new building paid for by public subscription and a donation from the Duke of Bridgewater. This Township School was situated on the appropriately named School Road (which started life as School Lane). In 1854 the school applied for conversion to a British School, which meant that children from all religious denominations could be taught there. By 1879 a new building had replaced this school, still on School Road, with places for 550 children. At the end of the nineteenth century the school was inadequate for the needs of the growing town. Attendance at school was not compulsory until the Education Act was passed in 1870, and after this date several schools were enlarged and more new schools were built. The Township School was replaced by a new elementary school built on Springfield Road, thus bringing it back full circle to the point where it started out. The school at Sale Lodge, founded in 1854 by Mr Howarth for the children of Sale Moor, was also converted to a British School. The National School, now St Anne's, on Trinity Road, for girls, boys and infants, was built in 1863-64, and the first master and mistress of the school were Edward Yates and his wife Mary.

For those who wished to continue their education after leaving school there was the library service, which began in the old Township School in 1887, founded by the Free Libraries Trust. This organization urged the council to adopt the Public Libraries Act, and set about raising the money to build a new library. The Free Library on Tatton Road was built in 1891, paid for by public subscription. Six years later the Technical School was built adjoining the library. This school was enlarged in 1903. The librarian was the organizing secretary of the Technical School, and the two establishments worked together. The library had acquired over 10,000 volumes within its first decade, and had a lending section as well as a reference department. The present library replaced this building in November 1938.

Housing schemes and new estates were prominent from the 1920s onwards. For those who could afford to buy their own homes, there were several opportunities, as new houses were built by private building firms. This was a feature of the years between the two world wars, when housing accommodation was provided almost exclusively by private developers, reaching a peak at one stage of nearly 1,000 houses per year. In that same period the Corporation built only 600 houses in total. In a report issued in 1955 it was calculated that there were 12,239 privately owned houses in Sale. These were perhaps mostly a product of the 1930s. The houses of the Moor Nook estate on Derbyshire Road South were advertised in a brochure issued in the 1930s by W.H. Matthews Ltd, a building firm based in Manchester. £25 secures you a house, proclaims the leaflet, with the telling remark 'be your own landlord and save money'. The total cost varied from £420 to £520 for a new house, depending on its size and design, of which there were eight basic choices. The brochure explained that the building firm, in collaboration with a leading architect, had evolved an Ideal Artisan's Home, situated in a charming residential district of character in delightful surroundings.

The layout was to permit no more than eight houses to the acre, and the streets were to be broad and lined with trees, with 'corner greens and shrubberies interspersed'.

In 1935, new semi-detached luxury homes built by Mauldeth Homes Ltd were advertised for sale on Washway Farm estate, convenient for the 47 and 48 buses, and priced at £374, with a deposit of £17 and three shillings, for type one houses, which comprised hall, lounge, dining room, scullery, larder, coal house, three bedrooms, separate bathroom and toilet, bay windows at the front, and with asphalt paths and space for a garage. Type three houses cost £434, and the show house was open daily from 9 a.m. to dusk.

Before the Second World War the largest housing estate in Sale was the development at Beech Farm, where 200 houses were built. After the war, there was a vital need for housing, and efforts were made to cater for this by the council, with schemes such as the new flats on Georges Road, opened in 1949. By the 1950s the council began to take stock of the housing position in Sale and appointed a special committee to prepare a report in November 1953. The committee found that 618 private building licences had been issued in the previous seven years since 1946, of which over 400 had been taken up by Sale residents. The lengthening waiting lists for council houses was causing concern in Sale, as in most other areas in the country, for the most part because after the Second World War 'the local authority was the only body to which people in need of a house could look'. The Housing Committee had begun to arrange for transfers of tenants to more suitable housing, and the council had completed the building of 936 dwellings since 1945, and 259 further houses were nearing completion in 1953. About 750 people were waiting for houses, which included those who would have to be moved under slum clearance programmes and those who were already housed but required better accommodation. The report followed these findings with a list of available land and the number of dwellings that could be accommodated on the sites. There were some problems, for instance, to the west of Manor Avenue, there could be no development until sewers were built and the extension to the sewage works was completed. Development here began in the 1960s by Manchester Corporation.

This house on School Road was used as the original municipal offices for Sale Borough Council from 1875-1914.

Woodhouse Lane, 1947, showing Ivy cottages, which were situated on the north side of Woodhouse Lane on the corner of Chester Road.

Left: Sale Cottage, Old Hall Road, was built around 1790. *Right:* Brighton Grove, 1920.

Sale Town Hall, 1915-16. The foundation stone was originally laid in May 1914 and the town hall was opened to the public in December 1915.

Terraced housing for the workers: this is Chapel Court, situated at the rear of Chapel Road. The property was known locally as Cabbage Row.

Buck Lane looking towards Church Lane.

Buck Lane, Ashton on Mersey, 1877. (Photograph courtesy of Mrs Hammond)

Cross Street and Dane Road Corner, 1900.

Sale Alms Houses, Worthington Road.

Brogden Grove in the 1900s, with rows of solid, well-built houses. Brogden Road can be seen on the right.

Thatched cottage on Church Lane, Ashton on Mersey. The house was demolished in the 1930s and Green Lane can just be seen on the left before the cottage.

Northenden Road looking from Sale station, 1877.

Glenthorn Grove, *c.* 1912. These stylish semi-detached houses were built sometime around this date and stood opposite a field which ran onto South Grove, a road which was unadopted. During the 1920s there was a gate here, which was always kept locked apart from one day a year.

The new housing scheme, Firsway, May 1980.

Opening of the council flats on Georges Road, 14 November 1949, by the mayor and Councillor F.H. Highley. After the Second World War there was a great shortage of housing, giving rise to new schemes such as this one.

Georges Road Flats, when no one had yet planted the gardens, 1950s.

Alston Avenue looking towards Walton Road.

Firs Road, 1963.

Harewood Avenue, 1963.

Clarke Mount, Church Lane, Ashton on Mersey. These were solid houses with decorative brickwork and the name set in stone under the dormer window.

Brook's Institute was built by W. Brakespeare in 1874 with money donated by William Cunliffe Brooks MP, to celebrate the jubilee of Queen Victoria. It was built as a reading room but was also used as a soup kitchen for the poor of Ashton. It fell into disrepair after the First World War until the council renovated it and opened it as a community centre.

Roebuck Lane, showing the last outside toilet in Sale, 1961.

Ashton upon Mersey School. This school was built on land given by the Earl of Stamford to the rector of St Martins in 1818. The pupils were fee paying and by 1833 numbered fourteen boys and thirty-eight girls. The school became known as St Martins school in 1896 when it was extended. Eventually the building became too small and the school moved to Wellfield Junior School in 1967.

The official opening of the Kitty Wheeldon Gardens, 1993. This accommodation was built on land owned by the Salvation Army. The site was formerly occupied by Warwick House.

Sale High School in the early 1900s. This school opened in 1897 as a high school and kindergarten for girls. Some boys were taken up to the age of eight. The kindergarten eventually ceased and the building became the High School for Girls.

Worthington Road Elementary School was designed for 700 pupils and had a large central hall and seven classrooms. Mr Slater, the first headmaster, is seen here with one 1928 class. The school was built in 1905 and it is said that it was the first council school in Cheshire.

St Joseph's Primary School, Hope Road, 1974. By 1900 a new purpose-built day school had been built. However, by 1940 it was declared unfit and the children were housed in various accommodation until permission to build a new school was given in 1975. The new school opened in 1977 next to the site of the old one.

Children at play at Tyntesfield Primary School, 1975. The land on which the original house was built belonged to a farmer called John Marsland. He sold it to Samuel Brooks who built Tyntesfeild on it. In 1956 the house was sold to AEI (Associated Electrical Industries) who in turn sold it to Cheshire County Council in 1968 to be used as a primary school.

The site of the old Township School on School Road, Sale, 1955. There are very early references to the Township School including one in a document dated 1667. The schoolhouse was said to have been two cottages belonging to two paupers called Barlow, who had these cottages taken over by the overseer at their death. A new school was built in 1800, financed partly by the Duke of Bridgewater and partly by public donations. This was re-floored and extended in 1861. In 1879 a new school was built to house the increasing population of children and eventually, Springfield Road School opened in June 1907.

Sale Central School for Boys, 1918. This school was opened in 1908 in the building that had been Sale Township School on School Road. In 1914 it moved to Ashfield Road to a new building. The first headmaster was Mr W.A. Loftus who stayed in the post until 1938 and who is remembered for his love of Gilbert and Sullivan Operas.

Boys High School, Woodbourne Road. Mr E. Lloyd Jones originally opened this school in the 1890s as a boys' day and boarding school. It occupied two sites, one on Wardle Road and one on Poplar Grove. In 1908 Manchester Grammar took the building over and used it as a prep school until 1935 when the site in Woodbourne Road was ready. There is an owl over the door, this being the symbol of Manchester Grammar School. In 1949 Cheshire County Council took the school over and it became Woodbourne Road Primary. It then became more commonly known as Brooklands Primary School.

Manchester Certified Industrial School for Girls, Northenden Road, 1983. This school was built in 1876 to accommodate 100 girls. It was certified 21 April 1877.

Barkers Lane School 1914-15. This school opened in 1896 and was to accommodate 300 children.

St Anne's Church of England School was built in 1863 on land previously belonging to Samuel Brooks. This photograph was taken in 1928.

St Mary's School, *c.* 1928.

Sale's first motor ambulance with W.R. Burke and Superintendent Royle. The fist ambulance in the area was probably a horse and cart as it is recorded in 1876 that a cover was bought for the cart. However by 1880 the ambulance could not met the needs of the population so a new horse-drawn vehicle was bought for £60. The sides of the new ambulance were frosted to give the occupants some privacy.

St John's Ambulance Brigade training with the fire brigade, *c.* 1939. The ambulance was called 'Algy' after the registration number ALG. The fire brigade ran the St John's Ambulance.

Sale and Ashton Fire Brigade, *c.* 1914. This photograph shows the first motor engine.

Sale and Ashton on Mersey Fire Brigade practicing outside the library, *c.* 1910. Sale Fire Brigade was formed in 1872, but in 1898 Sale combined with Ashton on Mersey to provide a joint fire brigade. A steam engine was also purchased in this year although horses were still used to pull the fire equipment.

Sale and Ashton Fire Brigade. The equipment shown in this photograph would still be horse drawn. The horses had to be brought from a nearby cab station from which they were borrowed.

The funeral of Superintendent John Johnson Hunt, Chief of the Sale and Ashton Fire Brigade who died due to injuries sustained at a fire at the Brooklands Hotel.

Sale and Ashton Fire Brigade in front of the old station doors behind the Town Hall and Library. Note the firemen are wearing brass helmets which were later abandoned due to safety reasons.

Four

Commerce and Industry

The most important commercial activity in Sale until the growth of the railway was farming and market gardening. As late as 1844 the Tithe Map and Apportionment Book show that the area was sparsely settled with scattered farms on winding lanes, divided by the Bridgewater canal, and bordered on the west by the Roman road that formed the boundary between Sale and Ashton on Mersey. The area was described in 1864 in these terms: 'the soil is of a rich sand and peat, very productive, and market gardening is carried on to a great extent'. Even the Ordnance Survey map of 1876 shows houses and gardens on School Road, which became the shopping centre by the early twentieth century.

The coal trade was well represented in Sale, thanks to the arrival of the Bridgewater canal. In the mid-1850s there were three companies represented in the town, the Bridgewater Trustees, at the Coal Wharf; George Darbyshire and Co. who dealt in lime as well as coal; and John S. Earle, coal merchant. By 1903 the last two companies had disappeared, either taken over or replaced by different companies. Clifton and Kersley Coal Co. Ltd had set up on Broad Road, supplying 'house coal direct to the consumer from our own collieries'. On Chapel Road there was the Wigan Coal and Iron Co. Ltd. Only the coal business of the Bridgewater Trustees remained unchanged. The area round what is now the town hall and the railway station must have been noisy and dusty to say the least. The coal companies on the wharves were complemented by a number of coal merchants in Sale who operated round about the canal area. Some of these were women, including Mrs Ellen Armstrong on Marsland Road, and Mrs Sarah A. Hodcroft on Egerton Street. The coal businesses had to compete with the gas and electricity companies, and by the second decade of the twentieth century, there was a noticeable decline; of the nine coal merchants listed in Sale in1905, five of them had disappeared by 1911.

During the nineteenth and early twentieth centuries other businesses were largely associated with horses, for instance in the second half of the nineteenth century John Allcroft ran a blacksmith's premises, there were three wheelwrights and one saddler and harness maker in Sale. The number of traders who dealt with all manner of things for horses increased towards the beginning of the twentieth century. As an idea of how utterly different the centre of Sale would have looked at the turn of the nineteenth and twentieth centuries, on School Road in 1905 there was a blacksmith's run by William Morton and two hay and straw dealers, run by Henry A. Gray at No. 24, and William Lowe at No. 40 School Road. Cross Street was another centre for horse owners, with two blacksmith's premises, a farrier, three hay and straw dealers, who were also listed under corn and provender dealers for horse fodder, and two wheelwrights, one of whom, Samuel Slack, was also a coach builder. Until 1906, you could purchase a horse in Sale from Arthur Twigge, who traded from Nos 37 and 57 Chapel Road, and also ran a cab and coach hire business at the same addresses. By 1907 his horse sales had ceased, and he ran his coach business from Victoria Mews, Mersey Road,

Ashton upon Mersey. For a short time he still lived at Chapel Road, but eventually moved to a house on Mersey Road. Another business associated with coaches was that of John Aldcroft, the only coach builder in Sale at No. 40a Tatton Road in 1898. By 1903 he had moved to Nos 55 and 55a Chapel Road. His business survived the end of the horse era, and transformed itself before 1913 to a motor car body builders, operating at the same address on Chapel Road. His was the only such business in Sale, all the rest being situated in Altrincham or Manchester.

Other trades were associated with building work, of which there was no lack after 1849 when the railway arrived; Luke Winstanley was listed in 1855 as a brickmaker and joiner, and there were several stonemasons. The beer and refreshment trade was represented by the Legh Arms, the Bull's Head, the Waggon and Horses, and in Ashton on Mersey the Buck, and the Old Plough. There were also a few beer retailers who were licensed to sell beer from their homes. Otherwise the list of trades in nineteenth century Sale reads like that of a small self-sufficient village, with a boot and shoemaker, tea dealers and grocery stores.

The amount of building that took place in Sale is illustrative of its rapid growth after the railway was established, and the influx of people needing houses, churches, schools, and shops. A directory of 1864 lists the new churches and public buildings; the Independent chapel in 1852; the church of St Anne in 1854, on a site given by Samuel Brookes; the Lodge School in 1854 and the National School in 1864. The population of Sale in 1848, according to a directory of the northern counties, was about 1,500, indicating that the census figures had not yet been instituted to produce an accurate count. By 1854 the population had risen slightly to 1,720, but only seven years later in 1861 the figure had risen to 3,031.

An increase in the number of people living in Sale engendered all manner of commercial activities to satisfy the daily needs of the new population. The early commercial establishments congregated on Cross Street, more the name of a district than a single street, where the passing trade went by on the main road to and from Manchester. This would be the focal point for shops, rather than the area now designated the centre of Sale. In the 1860s, if you needed remedies for colds and flu you could go to Cross Street to visit John Henry Goodwin, chemist and druggist, or perhaps to John Ellis who sold herbs; for food shopping, Peter Hewitt sold fruit and poultry, and Thomas Dodd dealt in fish, game and poultry. Adam Aldriga dressed tripe for resale, and the butcher's shop was run by John Westbrook. For shoe mending you would go to James Royle, who also sold china and glassware, and George Birkenhead dealt in fancy wares. There were representatives of trades that are now lost on Cross Street, such as Joseph Penney, saddler and harness maker, whose business would have been kept going by the number of farmers and carters in the area. On School Road, which was called School Lane at that time, there were far fewer retail businesses and more people who rendered skilled services. There was a furniture dealer, a coppersmith, a plumber, a joiner, a bricklayer, a cab proprietor, two milliners, three tailors, and a linen draper. For food shopping there was Charles Robinson, butcher, and Thomas William Davenport, grocer and tea dealer. Old maps show that the market place in the 1860s was near the canal, on Chapel Street, and by the canal there was a furniture dealer; a cabinet maker; Richard Ridyard, a coal dealer, and Ellison and Walters, grocers and drapers.

Shops on Northenden Road were well established by the late nineteenth century. Retail premises lined both sides of the road from Sale Bridge going towards Sale Moor, representing all types of business. There was a good choice of butchers' shops, grocery stores, clothing establishments, and a post office and newsagents, comprising a town centre nucleus on a larger scale than the remaining shops today. At the Sale Moor end of Northenden Road there was also a flourishing shopping centre by the late nineteenth century. The area around James Street and Hampson Street at the beginning of the twentieth century boasted grocery establishments, a chemist, an ironmonger's shop, a fruit shop, a florist, a glass and china shop, two drapers, one of whom shared the premises of the furniture dealer, and a stationery shop.

Industrial development was never very pronounced in Sale, except for the coal trade carried out on the wharves of the Bridgewater. As the population increased, service industries such as the post offices, gas and electricity supplies, sewage and waste disposal, road building and house building naturally increased along with the influx of new residents. Just prior to the 1920s, Fowler and Company, Scientific Instrument Makers, took over a building that stood between the canal and the town hall. The building had started out as a Congregational Chapel, and was converted in 1851 into the Wesleyan Methodist Chapel. In the 1950s a council report summed up the lack of heavy industry in the town: 'Sale is a residential borough, with a population of 44,000. Apart from a few comparatively small light industrial undertakings, together with the usual complement of shop premises, public houses, cinemas and the like, the whole of the rateable value of the borough is derived from residential hereditaments'. The report went on to say that the breadwinners of the Borough were employed in the industries of Broadheath and Trafford Park and other commercial centres.

Sale Palace was the first cinema in Sale. The building was originally Sale Public Hall, which was built in 1880. In the 1900s it was made into a roller rink, as roller-skating was very much in vogue at the time. In 1907 a stage was erected and it became a theatre, becoming known as the Palace around 1909 when films began to be shown there. It was famous for its smoky atmosphere and, because the floor was not sloped, the interruption of viewing as people walked to and fro from their seats crossing the light beam from the projector. Sale Palace was bought by Warwick Cinemas in 1947 and rebuilt in 1949. It became a repertory theatre which eventually failed. The building burnt down in 1962 and in 1964 the frontage was demolished.

The Savoy Cinema on Ashfield Road opened in 1913. It was demolished and rebuilt in 1928 to increase the seating from 700 to 1,300. The Union Cinemas procured it in 1936 and then the ABC chain in 1937. However, it did not change its name to ABC until the 1960s. It closed in 1977 after various changes and was demolished in 1985.

The Pyramid Cinema was the first 'luxury' cinema in Sale. John Buckley built it in 1933 on Washway Road. However, its license was not granted until 19 February 1934. There was some debate as to whether a cinematographic licence would be approved, as the police and owners of the adjacent properties put objections forward. However, the licence was granted and the first performance was eventually given on Monday 26 February. The designers of the cinema were Drury and Gomersall and it seated 1,940 people. The design was Egyptian, as the name suggests, and the cinema was awarded a plaque in the 1996 Cinema 100 celebrations to acknowledge this design. The cinema was bought by Rank in 1941 and taken over by Odeon in 1942. The last film was shown in October 1981. The building was listed in 1987 and was sold to open as Liberty's Discotheque in December 1990. It has recently been refurbished and opened as a gym called LA Fitness in April 2002.

The Woodcourt Hotel was built in 1896 on land purchased from the Earl of Stamford by Samuel Brooks in 1856. It was the largest of several great houses built on Brooklands Road and was occupied for some time by Nicholas Kilvert, lard manufacturer, together with his family and seventeen servants. In around 1919 the Kilvert family left the district, much to the regret of the parish, as they had been extremely active in the community. The house failed to sell until permission was received to turn it into a hotel in 1922. It thrived in this capacity until being recently demolished.

The Plough Inn is one of the oldest hostelries in the Sale area. In 1864 the landlord was Joseph Bradshaw. The Plough is well known as the place where Capt. John Moore first raised the Ashton on Mersey volunteers in 1803.

The Volunteer public house. The first documentation of this inn appears in two leases dated 5 February 1750, when James Massey sold a piece of land to John Harrison for £90. A public house was built on the land by 1807, originally called the White Lion. By 1827 the inn was known as the Volunteer. In 1865 the Volunteer changed hands, being sold by Hannah Dean to a brewer of Altrincham called John Astle Kelsall. When he died George Richardson and Benjamin Goodall bought it and held possession until 21 July 1890 when they sold it to Chester's Brewery Company Ltd of Ardwick. The brewery also bought the adjacent cottage and in 1897 both buildings were demolished and the present building erected on the site.

The Volunteer, 1924, with glossy-looking horses outside. In the age of horse transport, the building on the right of the hotel was used as a hayloft. It was later turned into a greengrocers when motorized transport superseded horse drawn vehicles.

The Buck Inn, which stands on the corner of Buck Lane and Green Lane, was built in the early eighteenth century. The ground floor windows and entrance door have been altered from their original state, and the pub has been extended. According to the *Sale Guardian* of 1958, Ashton Court Leet was held at the Buck and indeed the cellar on the right hand side of the entrance was used as a prison. The Inn is a listed building (1966) and contains the original large staircase. The stocks originally stood in the paved forecourt of the pub, before being moved to the churchyard.

The Bulls Head Inn as it was before rebuilding in 1879. George Hardy of the local brewery company purchased the land in 1878. Bass Charrington eventually took over Hardy's Brewery. In the 1900s bread, cheese and pickles were left on the counter together with clay pipes and matches. Customers could also save half a penny on a pint of beer by taking the wife into the snug!

The Brooklands Hotel, Marsland Road, in the 1920s. The hotel was built in 1872 and demolished in 1972. It was at one time owned by the Grand Hotel and was used as an annex whenever the Grand was fully booked. In 1934 it was bought by Chester's Brewery when it was well known for its food. According to Norman Swain, *A History of Sale*, it was here that the first agreement between employer and employee in the cotton industry, known as the Brooklands Agreement, was signed in 1893. A meeting was held between the Operative Cotton Spinners, and the Federation of Master Cotton Spinners, to try to come to some agreement in a dispute whereby the employers wished to cut wages by 5%. There was a strike, which the employers preferred to label a lock-out. The agreement reached at the meeting provided for tribunals to adjudicate between employees and employers.

Fowler and Co. were scientific instrument makers established in 1898, producing such things as calculators (not as we know them of course!). The building shown in this photograph is the old Congregational chapel into which Fowler's moved in 1919.The area at the front of the building was the site of the old Sale Market.

Left: Harold Fowler sitting at his desk at the Station Works in 1931. *Right:* Harold Fowler with two of his employees, who may be Eadie Batsford and Maggie Petrie.

Walkers Garage situated at the junction of Cross Street and Glebelands Road, probably around 1930. The garage closed in 1986.

Wright's Butchers on Greenhill Terrace, 1987. The name of the terrace can be seen above the Abbey National sign. The shop was situated on the corner of Green Lane and Greenbank Road, Ashton on Mersey. Note the air raid siren on the roof of the building.

R. Jones, Funeral Directors, Cross Street, Sale. The building is 'Eyebrow Cottage' which is supposedly the oldest cottage in Sale. It was built sometime between 1660-1680 and in 1806 was the home of Capt. John Moore of Sale who was famous for raising Sale Volunteers in 1803.

Thomas Bailey, fruiterer and fishmonger. This business, which was established in 1878, was situated at No. 95 School Road Sale from 1899. Orders were delivered and a price list issued first thing every morning. Lobsters, oysters and salmon were all available as well as a variety of seasonal fish.

John Hampson & Sons was a fruiterer and fishmonger situated at Nos 156-158 Northenden Road. This photograph was taken around 1875 and shows Mr Harry Hampson (left), John Hampson (centre left), Harry's brother John and Mr Leonard Aitkin (centre right).

John Woods Store, No. 170 Northenden Road at its junction with Marsland Road in 1903. This shop was one of the largest businesses in Sale. The building originally housed a blacksmith's forge and smithy, but in 1856 Thomas Wilkinson set up as a shopkeeper. Mr Wilkinson died in an accident and his wife married John Wood. The store provided a post office, bakery, grocer's and wine and spirit department and at one time delivered orders as far away as Chorlton. The horse-drawn delivery van can be seen on this photograph.

The original shop of Egginton & Son, c. 1924. The shop stood on Hope Road by the Brooklands Hotel. In the centre of the photograph is Mr G. Egginton Senior with two of his staff. At this time the son was an ardent short wave operator. The business was taken over by Rumbellows after the death of Gerry Egginton (Junior).

Vickers Coffee House, No. 103 Cross Street, 1912, showing Ted Sheffield aged five. The 1912 and 1913 Directories for Sale show Henry Sheffield, confectioner, to be living at this address.

Elizabeth's house furnisher, c. 1960. This shop stood at No. 78 Washway Road.

School Road, *c.* 1900. Boots cash chemist can be seen on the right.

Laying 'setts' in the road, *c.* 1900. Clarke Baker's shop can be seen in the background at No. 1 Cross Street. This was on the corner of Ashton Lane where the Magistrates Court now stands.

Ashton Lane around 1903 showing Clarke's shop at No. 1 Cross Street, displaying the fact that he was a tea and coffee merchant as well as a baker.

School Road looking in the direction of Washway Road; the side road opposite is Hereford Street. This photograph was taken from above the shop of Duncan & Foster Ltd (Pastrycooks) and although the date is uncertain it could be around 1940 as the railings were removed during the Second World War.

School Road, Sale, showing the Wesleyan Chapel on the left-hand side which was demolished in the 1960s. Boots Chemist is now on this site.

School Road, 1975, showing an old grain store or warehouse with hoist. The Corner Market used to be Gaskells.

Cross Street, Ashton on Mersey, with Dargle Road on the right. The cottages and terraced property is now the DSS building on the corner of Dane Road. Notice the tram in the distance.

The opening of the new sewage works extension at Sale, 1934. Sale was sewered in the 1870s, as the population had increased considerably. The 'privies' were emptied at night by night soil men but this became increasingly inefficient as the population grew. Brooks drain had been for some time the only means of drainage, and the North Cheshire Water Company provided the water for the scheme. Although £1500 was given, by 1900 another £1,000 was needed, as there was still 608 yards of Dane Road to finish. In 1931 a new scheme was started involving twenty-five acres of works, forty-eight tanks and nine miles of new main sewers.

Sale market, Christmas 1910. The market was situated on the forefront of Fowler and Co. at the side of the town hall. The building that was occupied by Fowlers can be seen at the back; it was once the Congregational church.

The pedestrianization of School Road as seen from the town hall end, 1982.

Five

Private Lives and Public Celebration

In the eighteenth century Thomas White, a medical doctor from Manchester, bought Sale Priory on Dane Road as his country residence. It was here that one of Sale's distinguished residents grew up to become one of the more important landowners in the area. Charles White was born in 1728, and when his father Thomas White died in 1776 he put up a monument to him, which was situated near a bridge over the Bridgewater Canal, known as Doctor White's Bridge. Unfortunately this monument was destroyed by accident in 1935. Charles followed in his father's footsteps and became a surgeon, and quite a distinguished personality. He was a fellow of the Royal Society, and a member of the Royal College of Surgeons, which originally started out as the Corporation of Surgeons. He was a co-founder of Manchester Infirmary with Joseph Bancroft and James Massey, and his improved procedures helped to reduce the death rate in maternity cases.

There is a macabre tale associated with Charles White, concerning one of his patients, Hannah Beswick. This lady was terrified of being buried alive, which was a not uncommon fear in the eighteenth and nineteenth centuries, when comas were not fully understood and tales of scratch marks found on the insides of coffin lids circulated wildly. Hannah asked Dr White to ensure that she should not be buried for a hundred years after her demise, just in case there was the faintest chance that she may not be properly dead. Charles White honoured her wishes when she died in 1757, keeping the embalmed body in his house. The body was removed to Manchester Museum for a short time, and eventually buried in Harpurhey Cemetery in 1868, so Hannah's last wishes that she should not be buried for a century were indeed realized – one hundred and eleven years after her death, and fifty-five years after the death of Charles White in 1813.

The White family were the pre-eminent landowners in Sale, laying claim to 256 acres in 1806, as John Newhill has shown in his book on Sale houses. As well as Sale Priory, Charles White owned Sale New Hall and Wallbank Farm. Through timely purchase the family built up their lands after Charles White's death until their holdings amounted to nearly 300 acres in Sale, as against the 166 acres of Samuel Brooks.

One of the most famous inhabitants of Sale was James Prescott Joule, who was not a native of the town but came to live on Wardle Road during the latter part of his career and the last seventeen years of his life. He was born in 1818 in Salford, and began his scientific studies under the famous John Dalton of Manchester. For a while he lived at a house called Thorncliff in Old Trafford, where he carried out his work connected with steam engines. He also began to experiment with the science of electro-magnetism and from his work in this field he discovered that the various forms of energy, mechanical, electrical and heat are basically the same – the essence of the first law of thermodynamics. He established that units of energy can be measured, and in this way his name has become a byword in everyday life, since the energy value of foodstuffs is now printed on tins and packets in Joules or calories (one calorie is roughly equal to four Joules). Like many eminent men of his time, Joule was a self-taught man who did not go to university to study, and so for some time he was not highly regarded in the academic and scientific world, but recognition came eventually. He won the Blue Ribbon of Engineering Science in 1852, and was made president of the Manchester Literary and Philosophical Society in 1860. In 1870 he won the Copley Medal, and then succeeded to the presidency of the British Association. He died 11 October 1889, and is buried in Brooklands Cemetery. There is a monument to him in Worthington Park.

The Brooks family was another of the landowning class whose memory is preserved in some of the buildings and place names in Sale. Samuel Brooks was a Manchester banker, who gave his name to Brooklands, an area of land that he purchased from the Earl of Stamford in 1856. He was responsible for much of the housing development in Sale. His eldest son William Cunliffe Brooks inherited a great fortune when Samuel died in 1864, and though some of the lands had been sold, there were still large areas of Sale in the bequest to William. The latter was a generous benefactor of Sale. He built Brooks Institute in 1888, and provided the fountain and water trough at the junction of Ashton Lane, Moss Lane and Barker's Lane. When horse-drawn vehicles were superseded by the motor car, the fountain impeded traffic, and was moved to one side so that it could be preserved. William gave the land on which St Mary's church was built, and in 1887, to commemorate the Golden Jubilee of Queen Victoria, he paid for the new tower at St Martin's, Ashton upon Mersey. He was one of the chief subscribers to the fund to build a Public Free Library in Sale, and he opened the Sale and Ashton upon Mersey Technical School, which was built next to the library in 1897. He was eventually knighted in 1886 and then died in 1897 in Scotland where he owned property at Glen Tana.

John Johnson Hunt was born in Tarporley in Cheshire and became the superintendent of the Sale and Ashton upon Mersey Fire Brigade, whom he served with distinction for over forty years, thirty of them with the Manchester Brigade. He retired from the Manchester service, but was appointed chief of the brigade when the Sale and Ashton Fire Services were amalgamated. He was awarded a silver medal while serving with the Sale and Ashton Brigade, having already been awarded Manchester and Salford Humane Society's silver medal with bar, for conspicuous bravery. Superintendent Hunt was tragically killed while fighting a blaze at the Brooklands Hotel in 1906. A portion of the roof fell on him as he inspected the premises, and though he was not killed outright, he died soon after from pneumonia. There was a glowing tribute in the newspapers explaining the circumstances of his death and describing the funeral service.

Another distinguished family was the Abercrombies who were native to Ashton upon Mersey. Sir Patrick Abercrombie was a world-famous town planner, and his brother Lascelles Abercrombie was a poet. A family that was not native to Sale but who made an impression upon the town was the Brogdens. John Brogden from Lancashire came to live in Sale in the 1820s. He founded the railway engineering firm of John Brogden and Sons, and although he was at first opposed to the establishment of the Manchester South Junction and Altrincham Railway, he won the contract to build it.

In more recent times, Sale was the birthplace of one of the foremost playwrights and Oscar winning screenwriters of the 1960s and 1970s. This was Robert Bolt, who was born in Sale on 15 August 1924. Three generations of the Bolt family, William and Ralph, Robert's grandfather and father, lived for some time at No. 13 Northenden Road, where they ran a furniture business. The family originally came from Chorlton, where Robert's older brother Sidney was born, but in the 1920s they moved to Sale. Robert was baptized at Sale Congregational Church on 19 October 1924. He was a pupil at Sale Preparatory School on Northenden Road, and then at Sale High School for Boys, then a subsidiary of Manchester Grammar School. In 1938, Robert transferred to the main Manchester Grammar School, and though he would be the first to admit that his academic career was not brilliant he went on to become a very successful playwright. His first play was performed in London in 1958, and his reputation was firmly established with *A Man For All Seasons* which won the New York Drama Critics Award in 1962, and was made into an Oscar winning film in 1966. Besides gaining other awards, the film established Robert Bolt as a screenwriter of excellence; he was awarded the Oscar for best screenplay. He went on to write the scripts for *Doctor Zhivago*, for which he won another Oscar, *Lawrence of Arabia*, *Ryan's Daughter*, *Lady Caroline Lamb*, *The Bounty*, and *The Mission*. He was closely associated with the director David Lean, and despite the fact that their relationship was not always a happy one, they produced fine work. Robert married the actress Sarah Miles in 1967. He suffered a severe stroke that almost took his speech away, but he continued to work after his illness. Robert Bolt died on 20 February 1995 and in 2001 Trafford Metropolitan Borough put up a Blue Plaque for him at his birthplace, No. 13 Northenden Road.

Public events in the Sale area include the various coronation ceremonies, the celebration of the end of the Boer War and the two world wars, and the Charter of Incorporation celebrations in 1935. This latter event followed the amalgamation of Sale and Ashton upon Mersey in 1930, under the title Sale Urban District. Preparations to obtain a Charter of Incorporation to create a Municipal Borough were begun soon after, and the application received the Royal assent in 1935. The brochure that was produced to mark this occasion proudly announces, 'The people of Sale will always be happy in the remembrance that it was in the Silver Jubilee Year of His Most Gracious Majesty King George the Fifth – when the four quarters of the globe resounded with joyous outburst of a great and abiding loyalty to the Imperial Throne – that they were honoured by this signal mark of the Royal Favour'.

For the benefit of residents and visitors the Municipal Borough maintained parks and gardens in the town, such as Worthington Park, named after Mrs Worthington who donated the land in 1900; a recreation ground in Ashton for football; tennis putting and bowls and Walton Park with two bowling greens and a tennis court. Sport was always well catered for in Sale, as a guide book to the town makes clear. There was angling on the Bridgewater canal, athletics with Sale Harriers, several bowling greens and cricket clubs, rugby was always a feature of the town, and swimming, golf, hockey and squash courts were available. Nowadays there is also Sale Water Park for various aquatic pursuits.

Sale Old Hall was at one time the residence of Sir William Bailey and his family. Sir William was a businessman and inventor. He served as an Alderman for Salford Council and was also president of the Manchester Literary and Philosophical Society. He was a prominent figure in the building of the Manchester Ship Canal Company and in 1894 was presented with a knighthood by Queen Victoria. His literary collection of books by Shakespeare and Montaigne were famous throughout Europe. This photograph taken in the grounds of Sale Hall, around 1900, shows the family outside the Togo pagoda, which was named after the Japanese Admiral Togo who took part in the Russian/Japanese war of 1905. The pagoda was constructed from material which had been used in The Manchester Royal Jubilee Exhibition of 1887.

The playwright Robert Bolt, seen on the left, was born in Northenden Road, Sale, on 15 August 1924. He spent the early part of his life in the Sale area where he attended the local school before moving on to the Manchester Grammar School. He is seen here with his friend, R. Puddephatt, when they were both members of the Boy Scouts. His first play was performed in London in 1958 and it was not long before he established a reputation for himself with the play *A Man for All Seasons*, which won the New York Drama Critics Award in 1962 and was later made into an Academy Award winning film in 1966, for which he won an Oscar for the screenplay. As a screenwriter his credits include *Dr Zhivago*, for which he also won an Oscar, *Lawrence of Arabia*, *Ryan's Daughter*, *Lady Caroline Lamb*, *The Bounty* and *The Mission*. He was married to the actress Sarah Miles and died on 20 February 1995. On 7 June 2001 a Blue Plaque was erected in Northenden Road, Sale, to commemorate his achievements. (Photograph Mr R. Puddephatt)

Left: Samuel Brooks was a successful commercial banker who was responsible for the development of large areas of housing in the Sale area. In 1856 he bought a large piece of uncultivated land from the Earl of Stamford and in 1859 began a project that was to result in the area we know today as Brooklands. One of his ambitions was to build a straight road from Brooklands station to Prospect House in Hale Barns; the road, which was to be four miles long, was never completed. *Right:* St Anne's church, Sale, 1900. The church was built on a site given by Mr Samuel Brooks. It was opened on 14 July 1854 and the registers date back to 1856. Seating was provided for up to 900 people yet despite this, in 1864 and again in 1887 the church had to be enlarged to accommodate the continued rise in urban growth.

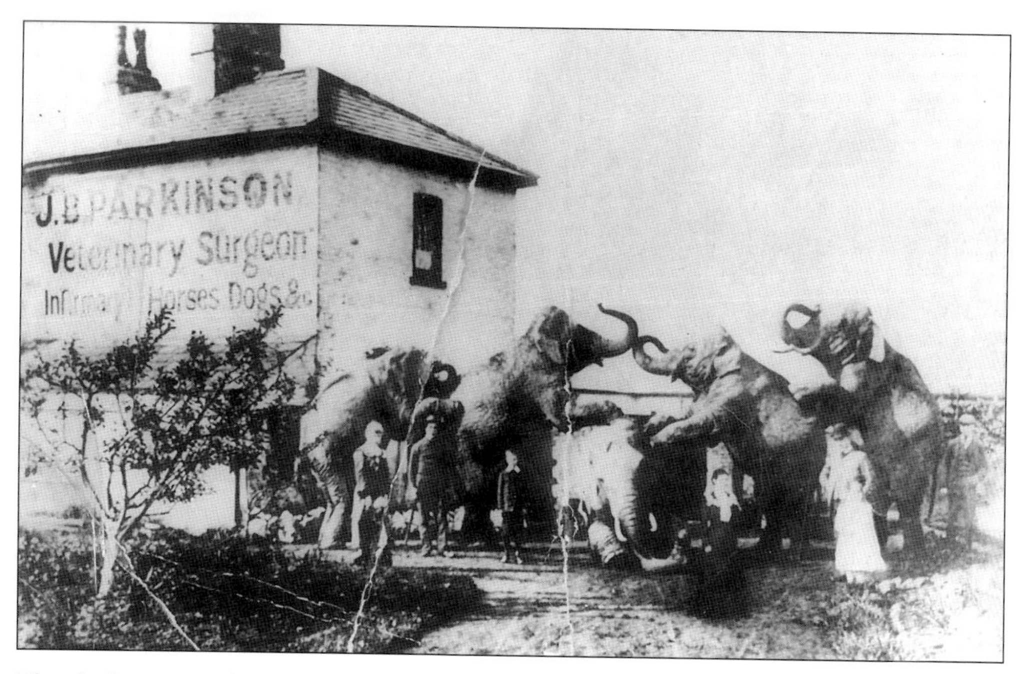

The elephants seen here were originally thought to be part of a show called the Savage South Africa Show. They took part in a procession to celebrate the end of the Boer War in 1902. A local story, which has been passed down, suggests that one of the elephants died on the route and was subsequently buried where it had fallen, somewhere in the Dane Road area of Sale.

Mr Alfred Higson founded the Sale and District Musical Society in 1907. The first concert was performed on Thursday 5 March 1908 in the public library in Sale. The choir was competitive and appeared in music festivals throughout the country, where they achieved reasonable success. In 1935 the choir triumphed at the Royal National Welsh National Eisteddfod at Caernarvon by winning first prize, which was then followed up by three further successes. In 1945 Mr Higson was made a Freeman of Sale and in 1947 the choir won the International Musical Eisteddfod in Llangollen.

The Coronation of George V on 22 June 1911 presented the country with a chance to celebrate. This photograph shows the members of the Trinity Methodist church in procession, going along Broad Road. In Sale, the coronation day began with services of thanksgiving; one was held at St Anne's church in Sale, while another one was held at the Congregational church. In the afternoon a procession of Sunday school children, headed by the Altrincham borough band, walked through the town before finally assembling in Sale Park, where a large assembly of people sang the national anthem. The centre of Sale was decorated with bunting and School Road, was spanned by pretty Chinese lanterns, which were illuminated during the evening to everyone's delight. Every child received a souvenir mug to celebrate the occasion.

The first Sale Carnival, held on 27 August 1921, was to raise funds for the Sale and Brooklands War Memorial Hospital. The Countess of Stamford attended the event, which proved to be a huge success. Everyone entered into the spirit of the occasion and the monster fancy dress procession was an overwhelming success. The carnival procession, which was led by the Congleton Town Prize Band left Sale Town Hall at two o'clock and proceeded via Ashfield Road, Cross Street, School Road, Northenden Road, Old Hall Road and finally Broad Road to Worthington Park where events such as competitions and displays took place. The day concluded with the Garnett's concert party, which took place at the town hall. *The Sale Guardian* newspaper reported on Friday 2 September 'the biggest and best organized open air event spectacular venture promoted in the Sale District for many years'. The photograph shows the motorcar procession, which took place as part of the main procession.

Sale Carnival looking towards Stretford, 1920s. The Reddish Jazz Band can be seen at the front of the procession, which has just passed the Bulls Head public house in the centre of Sale. (Photograph Mrs D. Vickers)

Sale Carnival with morris dancers, 1929. (Photograph Mr and Mrs Thorpe)

To celebrate the end of the Boer War a procession was held throughout Sale, Ashton and Sale Moor. People lined the streets to watch the parade, which included an ox and five elephants, which had been borrowed from the Savage South Africa Show for the occasion. The festivities included the roasting of the ox, which took place on a specially prepared spit in a field off Glebelands Road. Mr Henry Kilvert cut the first slice of meat before the ox was carved up and served. Schoolchildren from the area were each given a ticket, which entitled them to a slice of beef and a piece of bread, provided they brought their own plate to eat it from. This photograph shows the ox being paraded through the town prior to its unfortunate end.

The St Anne's Christian Brotherhood Bowling Green was opened on Saturday 22 May 1909. The land was leased from the Brooks estate for a five-year period for the sum of £15 and included an option to buy. The green was completed six months after the first sod had been cut and almost every house in the district had been canvassed to raise the necessary money to fund it. *The Sale Guardian* newspaper reported that 'The Chairman, in asking Mr William Mills to formally declare the green open and bowl the first 'wood' said that in that gentleman they had one who had served them as churchwarden, and one who always had the good of the parish at heart'.

To celebrate the Festival of Britain in 1951 an association football match took place between a Manchester United XI team and a Sale XI team at the gas board sports ground on Glebelands Road in Sale. The match resulted in a draw of 2-2. The Sale XI: Shelmerdine, Coane, Collins, Leyton, Stanford, Brownhill, McNamara, Cordingley, Hall, Taylor, Enright.

Manchester United XI played against Sale during the Festival of Britain in 1951: Wood, Lomas, Killin, Evans, Cope, Bent, Bradley, Clempson, Ritchie, Lewis, Bond.

The children seen here in the photograph are attending St Paul's Sunday school picnic, which took place on 26 May 1915 at Worthington Park in Sale. In the past the church played a more prominent role in everyday life than it does today and most children of all denominations attended their local Sunday school where they were taught religious studies. During Whitsuntide the children would take part in a procession of witness, throughout the streets dressed in their 'Sunday Best' in honour of the occasion.

Sale FC was originally formed in 1861 and is one of the oldest teams in the country. The records of the original club still exist in the form of a minute book, which is thought to be one of the oldest in the country. The early team players originated from Sale Cricket Club where they played on the cricket ground during the 'off season' in the winter months. It was due to the persistent efforts of Mr Alfred Ollivant, who recognized the need for a football club, that the club was created, although everyone thought he was mad to take the challenge on.

The entrance gates to Worthington Park during the early 1900s. Worthington Park was a popular place for the people of Sale. It was opened to the public on the 30 June 1900 and was originally known as Sale Park. It was renamed Worthington Park in 1949 as a way of ensuring that the original benefactress, Mrs James Worthington, will always be remembered in association with the park.

Sale Public Hall, Ashton Lane (1877) was at one time the home of Ashton on Mersey Council but during the early 1900s was used as roller-skating rink, which was popular form of entertainment at the time. When people began to lose interest in roller-skating, the hall was converted into a theatre before finally becoming a cinema which was known as the Palace. The Palace managed to survive into the early 1960s despite competition from the other cinemas in the area. It was destroyed by fire in 1962. (Photograph Mrs Hammond)

Ashton Park, between 1900 and 1910.

St Martin's church, Ashton on Mersey, 1877, before the addition of the tower, which was added along with a lych gate and a new vestry in 1887. In 1899 Sir William Cunliffe Brooks provided money for the tower and the vestry to be rebuilt.

The opening of the Wesley chapel on School Road. The chapel was built in 1860 to accommodate the rise in the Methodist congregation and was situated where Boots the chemist is today. Methodism was strong in the Sale and Ashton area and as the congregation continued to rise, the church had to be expanded even further. During 1884-85 an ambitious plan was undertaken to enlarge the building, which left the church in its final form and cost a total of £3,021.

The group of gentleman enjoying an afternoon bowling were all members of the Sale Queens Bowling Club. Seen here in the early 1900s, the gentleman standing in the centre of the group is Mr Wilfred Burke who was at one time the caretaker of Sale free public library.

Mr William Burke, who was the caretaker of Sale Library from 1905 to 1945. During his lifetime he also served as a fireman and an ambulance driver. He wrote down the memories of his life in the Sale area, a copy of which is held by Trafford Local Studies Centre.

A group of cub scouts who were members of the Third Ashton Pack, 1927. (Photograph Mr Sale, Queens Bowling Club)

Church of St John the Divine, Brooklands Road, 1877. (Photograph Mr T. Marriott-Moore)

Sale Moor Cricket and Hockey Club garden féte, 6 July 1912. The garden fete was an enjoyable way for clubs and societies to raise extra funds and was a very popular form of entertainment during the summer months. The féte here was held in the grounds of the cricket club, which was situated on Baguley Road. The Heyrod Street Old Boys Military Band who performed a selection of popular songs provided music, and there were sideshows and a fancy dress display. The day was a success and the club managed to raise the sum of £20.

Sale Moor Cricket and Hockey Club garden féte, 4 July 1914.

St Anne's Bowling Team, 1911, consisted of both ladies and gentleman and was considered a genteel form of sport.

The Sproston family during the early 1900s with their pony and trap, just about to set off on a journey.

During the early 1900s football was starting to become a popular sport both for players and spectators as people began to enjoy more leisure time than they had had in the past. The team seen pictured here in 1910 are Sale Moor Wednesday.

Sale and Ashton Fire Brigade taking part in the carnival, 1928.

Six
Times of War

The people of Sale and Sale Moor witnessed fragments of the major events that affected the country as a whole whenever there was a war. In the mid-seventeenth and eighteenth centuries there was military activity in and around the area, when the communities of Altrincham, Sale and Stretford were visited by troops of one kind or another. During the English Civil War Lord Strange's forces crossed the river Mersey at Ashton on Mersey ford on 23 September 1642, on their way to besiege Manchester. There was a threat to the safety of the realm when Bonnie Prince Charlie entered England at the head of his army in 1745, and though there was no fighting in and around Sale, Scottish troops came through the area, some of them demanding billets in Altrincham. No doubt the hostelries did good trade.

The effects of the Napoleonic wars were widespread across the whole country, especially after the failure of the Peace of Amiens, which was arranged between England and France in 1802. In 1803 an invasion by French troops was considered a very real threat, and there was a general call to arms. It is in this context that the Ashton upon Mersey cum Sale Loyal Volunteers was formed on 5 September 1803, by Capt. Commandant John Moore. This enterprising individual posted up notices in May 1803, designed to attract 'all lads of true Cheshire blood, willing to show their loyalty and spirit'. Meetings were to be held at the Plough Inn at Ashton on Mersey, or interested parties could apply to John Moore himself at Sale Hall. When the unit was formed, exercises took place on Sale Moor, where a splendid display was organized on 12 April 1804, when Prince William Frederick of Gloucester reviewed 6,000 volunteers. In 1978, Capt. Moore's uniform was restored and conserved at the North Western Museum and Art Gallery Service.

Documentation and photographs from the First World War tend towards the personal with family records, photographs of relatives in uniform and newspaper notices of deaths in the trenches. At Trafford Local Studies Centre, the photographic collection concerning the First World War is lamentably small, not least because the photographic habit was not as widespread in 1914 as it later became, and because the war was not brought directly to the town as it was in the years 1939 to 1945. Many more records survive from the period of the Second World War, when photographs can enhance the narrative. Before the outbreak of war central government and local government councils issued booklets and leaflets advising people what to do in the event of an air raid, and where to go for help. The councilors of Sale must have based their booklet on the one issued by Bolton council, since the typescript draft is entitled County Borough of Bolton, which is crossed out, and Sale is written over the top in ink. All the addresses are likewise amended, ready for typing up or type setting to be printed. The Medical Officer and Billeting Officer were both based at the town hall, while the Public Assistance Officer was housed at No. 1, Claremont Road. For some time before September 1939 when war broke out, Sale had been holding preparatory tests of its air raid precaution services, and when the air raids did not materialize, it was decided to continue with the Sunday practice sessions. The air raid wardens were concerned with blackout regulations, and a newspaper report of 8 September 1939 told how the police had been called to assist the air raid wardens in order to gain access to a house in Ashton on Mersey to put an outside light off. The war was only five days old at the time, so the inhabitants of Sale and Ashton would not have been accustomed to doing without lights.

Trench digging, erection of air raid shelters and sandbagging important buildings were begun with a will. Shelters were constructed in front of shopping centres such as those on Marsland Road and Woodhouse Lane East, 'for the safety of shoppers who may be caught in a raid'. The Welfare Centre in Chapel Road was to be used as the principal first-aid post, and the interior was remodelled to suit this purpose in 1939, at the same time as the exterior was being sandbagged. In preparation for gas attacks and chemical warfare, the public baths in Sale were to be used as the headquarters of the decontamination workers, of which there were thirty-two men, divided into four squads of eight men in each.

As food supplies diminished and rationing was introduced, the 'Dig for Victory' campaigns were launched across the whole country. Home food production in gardens and on any spare plots of land was actively encouraged, and leaflets and posters were put up to advertise the campaign. People were encouraged to keep poultry and rabbits to augment the food supply, though one wonders how many bunnies made it through the war because their owners could not bear to kill them, however hungry they may have been. Competitions, shows, talks and exhibitions were arranged to encourage people to grow vegetables. In February 1943 a whole week's programme of events was organized in Sale, beginning with a popular radio show of the time, called the 'Brains Trust' where a panel of experts gave advice on all manner of home food production. The 1942 growing season had been plagued by various insect pests, so Dr J.H Weston, adviser on mycology at Manchester University, was invited to the radio show to help with these problems. There was also an exhibition at the town hall, where advice was given by staff from the Cheshire School of Agriculture, and the Royal Horticultural Society set up stands with photographs and leaflets.

The possibility of an invasion was never forgotten, and on 23 February 1942 there was a meeting at Sale Town Hall to discuss the problem of food supplies during an invasion. The minutes of that meeting state that 'we are met to consider an event which we all hope will never occur and to make provisional arrangements which we hope will never have to be put into effect'. Local councils were responsible to the Ministry of Food, whose local representative was chosen from the officers of the council to liaise with the central government. At the meeting in February 1942, it was decided that the first priority in the event of an invasion of Britain was to organize a fair distribution of the available food, for which purpose it was essential to know the numbers of people in need of food, and the supplies that were stocked in all the shops in Sale, so that 'there must not be any possibility of the well-to-do buying up everything that money can buy and leaving the poorer members of the community without'.

One of the features of the whole of the war was the institution of savings campaigns to provide money for armaments, ships, and planes. All over the country money was raised at special events and by continued hard work by the campaigners. In November 1939, only two months into the war, there was a meeting at the town hall to set up the Savings Committee in Sale. The town was particularly successful in raising money. By the end of 1940 the amount of cash collected was about £470,000. In the first campaign War Weapons Week, the target of £125,000, enough to buy six bombers, was far exceeded, and the eventual total was nearly £316,000, enough for sixteen bombers. The posters did not mince words 'a bomber a day to keep Jerry at bay'. Other campaigns followed, Warship Week in March 1942, Wings for Victory in May 1943, and Salute the Soldier in March 1944. As a result of the warship campaign, Sale raised £316,000, and adopted HMS *Walker*, one of the 'V' and' W' class of destroyers. The ship was commissioned at Devonport in 1939, and in June 1940 took part in the naval operations off Norway, and was the last ship to leave Narvik as the evacuation took place.

The air raids on Manchester had as principal targets the vast works at Trafford Park, the docks of the Ship canal and the various factories of the suburbs. One of the most dramatic moments in wartime Sale was shared by the communities all around Manchester, in the blitz of December 1940. These particular air raids began on 22-23 December, when the air raid warning lasted from 6.35 p.m. on the 22 December until 6.35 a.m. on the morning of the following day. The bombers returned the next night, and on this occasion the town hall at Sale was hit by incendiary bombs. The roof and the interior were demolished and remained in this state until there was time and money after the war to resurrect the building.

During the Napoleonic wars on Thursday 12 April 1804 there was a review of the Volunteers on Sale Moor, 'at half past ten in the forenoon' by Lt-Gen. Prince William of Gloucester. A programme was drawn up prescribing the formation: the Cavalry on the right of the line, the Artillery on the left of the Cavalry, the Rifle Corps on the left of the line and the Pike Men on their right. The artillery was to fire a Royal salute on the approach and exit of the Prince.

Sale Volunteers in the 1880s.

The ox roast in Besson's Field, 1902.

At the end of the Boer War elaborate celebrations were attended by the people all over the country. In Sale, an ox roast was held, and this photograph shows the procession on the way to the roast, pausing outside the Waggon and Horses on Cross Street.

Long loaves (on the left) at the ox roast.

The 10th Cheshires, on a card posted from Brighton in 1915, and donated to the library by the Sproston family. The message on the reverse reads, 'Dear Mary, I don't know whether you can tell me on this, it is rather small... We have all removed from Boscombe station... with love from uncle'.

John Sproston in 1916.

Jack Derbyshire from Ashton upon Mersey, 1915.

Ralph and Leah Bolt, parents of the playwright Robert Bolt.

Preparing for the Second World War: sandbags in front of the library, September 1939. Note the gas mask carried in its box by the lady about to enter the library.

Workers continue to build the sandbag wall on the left of the library door.

SALE DIG FOR VICTORY WEEK

More Questions are Wanted

FOR THE **BRAINS TRUST**

At SALE TOWN HALL on MONDAY, 22nd FEBRUARY at 7-30 p.m.

Question Master: Mr. RAYMOND GLENDENNING of B.B.C. and Radio Allotment fame, with a panel of well-known experts.

ADMISSION FREE **Send your questions at once to the Question Master, c/o Town Hall, Sale.**

THE EXHIBITION

Opens WEDNESDAY, 24th FEBRUARY, at 2-30 p.m. and will remain open until 9-0 p.m. and thence daily 10 a.m. to 9-0 p.m. up to and including SATURDAY, 27th FEBRUARY.

FILMS, DEMONSTEATIONS, POULTRY, RABBITS, ETC. **ADMISSION FREE**

In order to provide more food as rationing began to bite, people were encouraged to dig up their flower gardens to plant vegetables. The Dig for Victory campaigns were encouraged by means of displays, exhibitions, posters, and in this case in Sale by radio broadcasts.

The tremendous air raids on Manchester and the surrounding towns in December 1940 caused damage in many towns surrounding the city. The main attack came on the night of 22-23 December, when the air raid warning lasted from 6.35 p.m. on the 22 December until 6.35 a.m. on the morning of the following day. The town hall at Sale was hit by incendiary bombs on the night of 23-24 December 1940, leaving a roofless shell, as can be seen here.

Sale Town Hall, still minus its roof and most of the interior, 1943.

War Charities were set up to provide money to buy armaments and equipment for the war effort. The titles Warship Week, Salute the Soldier, and Wings for Victory, all speak for themselves as to which branch of the service the money was intended to assist. This photo shows the members of the Sale Savings Committee around 1944. The committee was formed in November 1939, and the members of the committee organized a savings week a year before the project was taken up on a national scale.

Post-war reconstruction of the town hall in the 1950s.

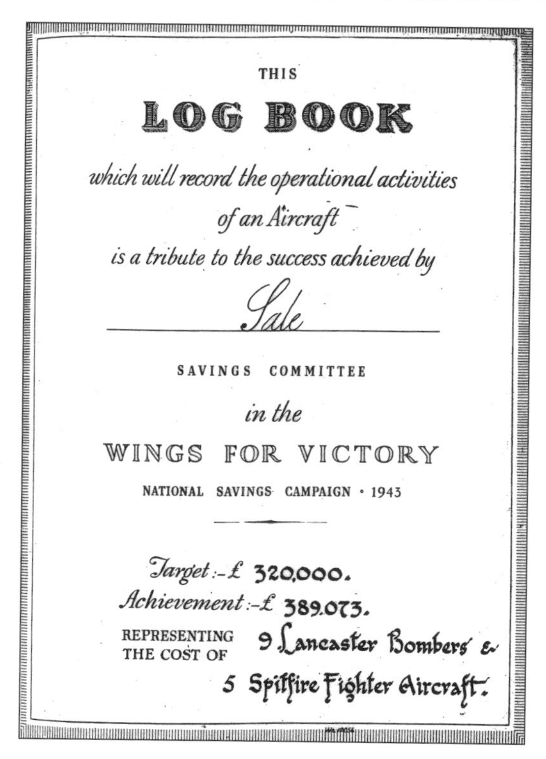

THIS

LOG BOOK

which will record the operational activities

of an Aircraft

is a tribute to the success achieved by

Sale

SAVINGS COMMITTEE

in the

WINGS FOR VICTORY

NATIONAL SAVINGS CAMPAIGN • 1943

Target:-£ 320,000.

Achievement:-£ 389,073.

REPRESENTING THE COST OF 9 Lancaster Bombers &

5 Spitfire Fighter Aircraft.

Left: The target for Wings for Victory Week in Sale in 1943 was exceeded by several thousand pounds, as shown by this page from the log book of one of the planes sponsored by Sale. *Right:* Posters advertised the savings for bombers with this little jingle: 'A bomber a day keeps Jerry away.'

Poster advertising Warship Week in 1942.

The ATC contingent marching from the station past the First World War cenotaph, during Salute the Soldier Week in 1944.

Marching past the ruined town hall during Salute the Soldier Week in 1944.

Inspection of the Home Front in the 1940s by Gen. McDougall.

The WAC of the US army took part in the Salute the Soldier Week parade.

The WRNS marching past the Town Hall in 1944.

A contingent from the US Army carrying their flag during Salute the Soldier Week.

The RAF band during Salute the Soldier Week.

Another US Army contingent in front of the town hall in the Salute the Soldier parade in 1944.

The air raid wardens played an important part in safeguarding communities against air attacks, assessing damage done by raids, and in reporting upon casualties and destroyed buildings. Their duties were outlined in handbooks and pamphlets issued by the central government, and local councils issued their own lists of officers appointed to First Aid Posts, firewatching duties and so on. Here the Sale air raid wardens take their place in the march during Salute the Soldier Week in 1944.

Children watching the parade during Salute the Soldier Week in 1944.

The Sale Home Guard on parade night in 1941. The fear of a German invasion was felt very strongly during the first years of the war, and a second line defence was formed from groups of older men, some of them veterans of the First World War. The Sale Home Guard used to assemble in an old cottage near Dainewell Farm, and issued a magazine called the *Dainewell Sentry*. These men performed their day jobs and then went on to do night duties and exercises at their appointed times.

The fire services performed over and above the call of duty all through the war, often in doubly dangerous circumstances while raids were still going on, and buildings were crashing down. This is the South Auxiliary Fire Service at Sale in 1939 or 1940.